Freya

Written by John Chalmers and Sandra Marrs

Collins

CHAPTER 1

Freya lived with her father, Campbell, chief of the Clan MacDonagh, in Curdoyne Castle on the shores of Loch Brannoch.
Her great-grandfather had laid the first stone. Tomorrow would be the annual competition, and as she had just come of age,
Freya would be taking part.

Tomorrow is a big day.
The competition, it means a lot.

I know, dad.

You don't have a brother, Freya.

I don't mind.
We have each other.

But one day the responsibility of clan chief will be on your shoulders.

And you know, my darling, there will be some voices that will speak against that.

It's your chance to show everyone that you will make a worthy successor.

But dad! I just want to enjoy the day.

Of course! But now that you have come of age, all eyes will be on you.

Freya thought about her father's words. She always loved the competition. But she could not shake a troubled feeling.

Surely everything would be fine. After all Cousin Anne would be there, and they were more like best friends than anything else.

They would often meet at the old oak tree and share their secrets, hopes and fears.

Of course, there would be Cousin Ranald too. He didn't like it when Freya and Anne did better than him in training.

There would be the archery that she loved so much.
From age five the bow and arrow had felt like an extension of her arm.

There would be the sword fencing her father had taught her.
She could beat anyone with her wooden sword.

And there would be her favourite: close combat. To her it felt like a dance, and she had learned to use her speed and strength.

Quick as a fox, with a shock of red hair, she was her father's daughter.
Freya: a Norse god in name.

There would be swimming too. Crossing the loch several times a day was a way to build character, her father had said.
He was the strongest swimmer of all and made it look effortless.
Her cousins listened carefully to him. Listened and learnt.
Freya loved to race across the icy waters. Anne was never far behind.

They would also race each other in the castle. Freya knew every irregular step by heart and could run up and down the spiral staircase with her eyes tightly closed.

But as she woke the next morning, she did not suspect that her life was about to change.

It was the day Anne brought her the terrible news.

Freya! Something terrible has happened!

CHAPTER 2

One of Ranald's helpers unrolled a long linen scroll. He began to list the charges against her.

The accused is charged ...

... with having cast a spell on the grain, causing a great lightning storm, calling up a plague by witchcraft ...

Freya listened to the long list of accusations. She could not believe what she was hearing.

Witchcraft! You must be joking!

Her wrists were caught in the iron loops, the metal digging into her flesh.

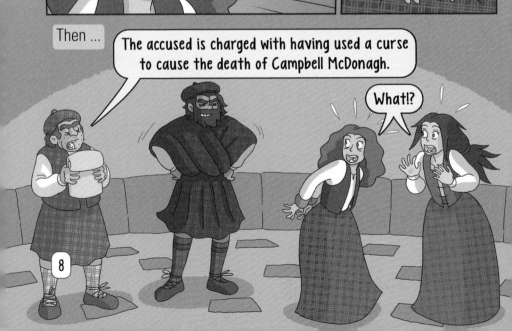

Then ...

The accused is charged with having used a curse to cause the death of Campbell McDonagh.

What!?

Kill my own father? I loved him!

But her words fell into the emptiness of the loch. Her kinsmen were seized by a wild-eyed frenzy. Their ears were closed to reason.

Freya has her greedy eyes on the position of clan chief!

She could not wait for her father to pass away naturally.

We will celebrate the life of the chief after one moon. The witch is forbidden to attend and must be imprisoned.

Freya could feel the eyes of her clan burning into the back of her head. She could barely understand their words.

Vile creature!

Witch!

Freya was moved to the castle dungeon awaiting trial.
There would be no competition day and a hearing was set for
three moons. Her cell was cold and dark and she felt all alone.

I must get out of here!

She watched the celebration of her father's life through eyes
full of tears and prison bars. It felt wrong not to be there.

Everyone, her whole clan, was gathered round the funeral pyre.
As she watched, she noticed Ranald slowly making his way to
the back of the crowd.

Ranald! You scoundrel!

Anne had also kept an eye on Ranald.
She followed him, watching from the shadows.

What is he up to?

Carefully she stayed out of sight, as he made his way up the spiral stairs.

He sneaked into the late chief Campbell MacDonagh's room.

Now this is what I was looking for.

Chief Campbell had left the deed box for his daughter, to be opened by Freya in the event of his death.

Ranald opened it to discover a letter and a bag of coins.

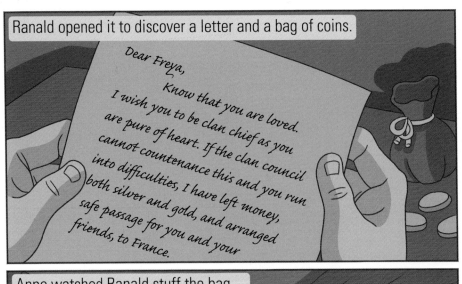

Dear Freya,

Know that you are loved. I wish you to be clan chief as you are pure of heart. If the clan council cannot countenance this and you run into difficulties, I have left money, both silver and gold, and arranged safe passage for you and your friends, to France.

Anne watched Ranald stuff the bag of coins in his own pocket. She stifled a cry as he threw the letter, intended for Freya, into the fire.

She won't be needing this.

She waited until Ranald had left the room, quickly doused the flames and snatched the letter.

Oh my! Freya is in terrible danger. I need to speak to her.

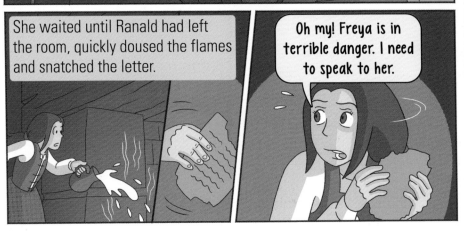

CHAPTER 3

The trial was a farce. Freya couldn't seem to get her voice heard. Nobody listened to her. Anne demanded justice to no avail. Ranald had the support of most of the clan, and superstition reigned. Worse, Anne couldn't even speak to her friend. Freya was too closely guarded.

Campbell McDonagh was a popular and respected chief, but he did not father a son ...

... and so Freya would be his successor even though it would be highly unusual to have a female chief. However, given the serious allegations of witchcraft against her ...

Of course, I'm not a witch! Witches don't even exist!

Bluster! Bluster! Bluster!

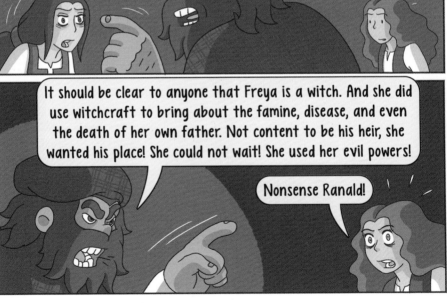

If she could call up all those terrible things, she could free herself of her shackles! She's no more of a witch than I am!

Anne's sister, Jeanie, looked around fearfully.

Don't get involved Anne: they'll brand you as a witch too!

You know the price! They've been burning witches. Remember North Berwick! On the beach! Three stakes! It would be a fool that gets involved! And for what? A female chief? Whoever heard of the like?

For goodness sake, listen to yourself! She's our own kin! We're supposed to be in this together!

We need to help her somehow!

Silence!

15

And so a pyre was built around a stake, and Freya had to watch this awful process from behind her prison bars.

CHAPTER 4

Sunset brought a feeling of dread to the glen. The decision sat very uncomfortably on the shoulders of the clan council. Oh, how they missed the wisdom of their chief. A father would never allow his daughter to suffer such indignity. Somewhere through the gathering dusk a melody did swell. A plaintive song.

Almost by instinct Freya knew to go to the window. With her ear to the bars, she heard a forced whisper.

Freya! I need to speak with you!

Later, when night had fallen, Freya's guards heard a strange sound.

Freya's guards were alarmed by the dreadful ghostly noise. At first, they stood shivering, petrified with fear.

Eventually they decided to investigate.

Do you think the witch summoned a ghost?

Anne had sneaked in and was hiding behind them.

Freya? I don't know about that.

But don't they say the castle is haunted?

As the guards opened the door to Freya's cell, Anne readied her rope.

They were shocked at what they discovered inside.

... then locked them in the prison.

Quick!

Freya whispered to her friend.

This stays our secret, Anne! My father showed me this hidden door when I was but a child.

She pushed on the prison wall and a small stone door swung open.

A secret passageway!

They closed the door behind them and began their escape.

They'll never find us here.

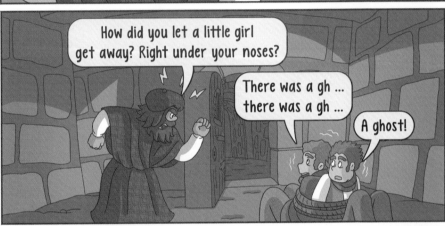

And so Ranald formed a search party with torches and swords and they started stalking across the glen. Dogs were given Freya's scent and began to sniff the gorse and heather.

CHAPTER 5

Progress through the secret passageway was uncomfortably slow. Their way was narrow and the stones were covered with damp slippery lichen. Cobwebs crept across their faces making it impossible to see. Down and down they crawled into the darkness. Wind howled and whistled through the cracks in the old stone walls.

Are you sure this is the right way?

Shh! Best be careful. Don't make a sound!

Deep down beneath the castle they came to another concealed door. But as they tried to open it ...

... suddenly, inexplicably, a flood of water swirled around them.

Something was blocking the mechanism. The door refused to move.

Perhaps the workings had eroded over time? Rust or decay? The slipstone refused to budge. Not even with all their combined effort. Pushing and pushing.

The water pressure was too great, and the level was rising rapidly. Soon, they would be trapped. A watery end.

Freya had an idea. Together they shoogled the stone a little, back and forth. It took agonising, long seconds, but then there was a click. "Try it now!" Freya said, and Anne did. This time the great stone eased open.

click

At last, they were in the loch.

Suddenly, fear paralysed them completely.

What dreadful creature was this? A huge lurking shadow of a shape. Something terrifying from the silent, black depths of the loch. An ancient creature from below. A flash of teeth. A terrible long neck.

Meanwhile, on the moor, Ranald was getting nowhere.

Now, if the dogs can't pick up her scent, I have an idea.

He consulted the local clairvoyant.

Well, can you see anything?

The picture is getting clearer.

They're in water ... swimming in shallow water ... water all around them.

Oh no! It's terrible! A monster! That's not possible!

Oh, I know exactly where they are. They'll never survive this.

CHAPTER 6

Freya and Anne were swimming as fast as they could. The enormous monster was on their heels. But the beast was slow and they had had years of training.

By swimming close to the bank, among the shallows, they had managed to keep the creature at bay.

The monster's hideous mouth was about to grab them ...

... but in the nick of time, gasping for breath, at last, Freya and Anne scrambled up the bank.

It had tentacles! I'm sure it did.

Its tail went on forever. I swear!

Oh Anne! There really is a monster in the loch!

I always knew it. I have sensed it. Sensed it watching me many moons.

Anne! Thank you! I couldn't have escaped without your help.

Listen Freya! I saw Ranald steal a letter and coins that your father had intended for you!

But I managed to rescue the letter. Your father left you instructions so you can escape.

The ink had almost vanished underwater, but Anne had memorised the letter by heart and told Freya everything.

Come on we can't stay here! It isn't safe!

Suddenly, there was a flicker of torchlight and angry shouts. Ranald and his men were upon them.

There she is! Get her!

It's the witch!

31

CHAPTER 7

At first Freya and Anne were caught completely by surprise.

In an instant, Freya regained her composure and with a swift kick saved Anne from the point of an unfriendly sword ...

... and dealt with the three assailants.

The women were quicker and more agile than their pursuers. Freya threw the white sheet over the attackers.

Climbing trees came naturally to Freya. She knew the best way up each and every one. The woods had been her playground as a child.

In no time she and Anne were high in the branches and heading off across a familiar path through the air, leaping from tree to tree.

Ranald shouted up a tree. Two hawfinches watched him from a hollow in the trunk.

Through the night air, Freya and Anne heard the sound of barking and howling. They had defeated Ranald this time, but he was now on their trail and he was using the dogs.

CHAPTER 8

Anywhere beyond the glen was potentially dangerous. Treacherous unknown land. Sinister strangers. Not to mention the fact that 16th-century Scotland was a turbulent place. Europe was not long out of the Dark Ages and the Reformation had thrown society into turmoil. Warring armies roamed the heather. Ahead of them to the left towered Ben Larrish, and to their right lay moor … rough land that was uneven underfoot with hidden bogs.

Freya had to stop for Anne.

My heart is going to burst.

Sit down and breathe slowly.

We'll have to make the journey to France, like my father wrote in his letter.

I can't believe we have to flee our own home!

You'll have your day, Freya, but for now my breath is back, and we should be getting on.

Two tiny figures, silhouettes against the silver moon, Freya and Anne threaded their way carefully across the moor.

Even though the upland was deserted, a vast open space, the girls found themselves whispering. Speaking to each other in hushed tones.

How did my father know there would be trouble?

Your father was a wise man. He could see deeply into people.

There didn't have to be a problem with making you chief. This witchcraft thing is eating everything from the inside.

As the moon is my witness, I've never made a curse in my life.

Of course you haven't, Freya. Don't let them make you doubt yourself.

CHAPTER 9

Anne followed Freya across the moor as she ran towards the rocky outcrops that lay at the foot of Ben Larrish. Ranald and his men approached them at a frantic pace.

Follow me! We'll be able to lose them in the rocky paths.

They won't be able to swing their swords properly in the narrow cracks.

Freya was right, the rocks made it hard for Ranald and his men to attack them. But there wasn't much space at all, and the girls had the terrible feeling they were running out of time.

Ranald was left clutching thin air. He was raging but he was far too scared to jump.

Freya and Anne crossed a stream. The water would put the dogs off their scent. And it felt good to cool down.

But their pursuers were close and now there was nowhere to hide.

Freya and Anne held their breath. Could they stay hidden under their plaid? Was this the end?

CHAPTER 10

Ranald and his men had walked straight past them. Freya and Anne could see them disappearing over the horizon, way off track.

We'll be safe for a little while.

Far in the distance the girls could see a small dwelling place. Pale smoke curled up in the early morning air.

Maybe someone is living there?

Well, that's no good. We need to be careful not to be seen.

But maybe they could help us? I don't know if I can go on like this. My legs are getting heavier and heavier.

Freya had to make a difficult decision. They were getting worn out and it had been a long night. Clearly, her cousin Ranald had spies everywhere; it seemed like they were always two steps ahead of them. It was terrifying. Escaping prison was an admission of guilt. If they were caught, Anne was done for too.

They were both so thirsty. There was only time to drink a little from the stream before they had gone into hiding.

A young couple opened the door to them. They seemed friendly. But could Freya and Anne really trust them?

Inside the cottage was warm. A relief after the harsh cold of the night air.

Sit down and rest your legs. Break some bread with us.

We don't have much but wouldn't see you go hungry.

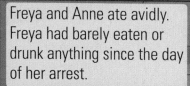

Freya and Anne ate avidly. Freya had barely eaten or drunk anything since the day of her arrest.

Where are you travelling from? Are you going far?

Heather and I are just starting our life together.

You can stay here and gather your strength. You look worn out and thin.

A distant barking reached their ears, piercing the stillness of the house. It was the dogs!

Freya felt her skin crawl. She looked at Anne. The poor soul had turned grey and was shivering with fear. They had to do something, or else ...

Ranald and his search party had turned back.

There! Let's look in that cottage!

The fugitives barely had time to escape through the back window, much to the surprise of their hosts.

Ranald saw the young couple; they'd come out of their house to help. Where they pointed, he could see two small figures running frantically in the distance.

And they ran after them, picking up the pace.

Across the moor they ran, two tartan skirts against a pale morning sky.

At first, they managed to keep a good distance between themselves and Ranald, but as time passed, they grew tired and began to slow down.

Then they came to an impasse. Ahead of them: a cliff edge. They could go no further.

Finally, they were trapped.

The two figures were in fact the young married couple disguised as Freya and Anne. They had switched clothes! The man still had his full beard.

Still refusing to believe that he had been played, Ranald pulled frantically at the man's beard ...

That's impossible! Reveal yourself Freya!

... until the man finally thumped him.

Meanwhile, far away, Freya and Anne were running free across a beach, the destination intended by Freya's father.

Oh Anne, we tricked him! There's dad's boat! The safe passage he wrote about in his letter.

Campbell MacDonagh had provided safe passage for his daughter after all.

The girls would need more luck in time as a long voyage would change them.

And without Campbell's silver and gold they would have to work their passage. But their small boat made its way across the sea to a tall ship ready to take them to France just as her father had promised. They set sail leaving the past behind.

EPILOGUE

Months, years passed. Freya and Anne had settled in France and made new friends and a new life. It hadn't been easy, and they had missed their home. Then one day they received a letter.

It was from Cousin Jeanie. She was writing with good news.

Freya read it, weeping tears of joy.

Freya was exonerated and returned home to Scotland with Anne. Attitudes were changing and people were no longer hunting witches. Too many women, men and children had been falsely accused. Freya took her rightful position as new clan chief and Anne always had her back.

Freya's emotion journey

quick-witted

resourceful

determined

unsure

relieved

55

✿ Ideas for reading ✿

Written by Gill Matthews
Primary Literacy Consultant

Reading objectives:
- recommends books that they have read to their peers, giving reasons for their choices
- ask questions to improve their understanding
- draw inferences such as inferring characters' feelings, thoughts and motives from their actions, and justifying inferences with evidence
- predict what might happen from details stated and implied
- summarise the main ideas drawn from more than one paragraph, identifying key details that support the main ideas

Spoken language objectives:
- use relevant strategies to build their vocabulary
- articulate and justify answers, arguments and opinions
- participate in discussions, presentations, performances, role play, improvisations and debates

Curriculum links: Relationships education: Caring friendships

Interest words: outraged, grieving, quick-witted, resourceful, determined

Build a context for reading

- Ask children to look closely at the front and back cover of the book. Discuss when and where they think the story takes place.
- Focus on the word *tentacles* on the back cover. Support children in working out the meaning of the word.
- Point out that this is a graphic novel. Explore children's knowledge of graphic novels and their typical features.
- Ask children to turn to pp2–3. Discuss the order in which the boxes should be read. Ask what the difference between the text in speech bubbles and the text in blue boxes is.
- Challenge children to find out from these pages when and where the story takes place.